The Book of Praise

Derwin Boyd

The Book of Praise
Trilogy Christian Publishers
A Wholly Owned Subsidiary of Trinity Broadcasting Network
2442 Michelle Drive
Tustin, CA 92780
Copyright © 2022 Derwin Boyd
All rights reserved, including the right to reproduce this book or portions thereof in any form whatsoever.
For information, address Trilogy Christian Publishing Rights Department, 2442 Michelle Drive, Tustin, Ca 92780.
Trilogy Christian Publishing/ TBN and colophon are trademarks of Trinity Broadcasting Network.
For information about special discounts for bulk purchases, please contact Trilogy Christian Publishing.
Manufactured in the United States of America
Trilogy Disclaimer: The views and content expressed in this book are those of the author and may not necessarily reflect the views and doctrine of Trilogy Christian Publishing or the Trinity Broadcasting Network.
10 9 8 7 6 5 4 3 2 1
Library of Congress Cataloging-in-Publication Data is available.
ISBN: 978-1-68556-699-9
ISBN#: 978-1-68556-700-2 (ebook)

Table Of Contents

Stand Your Ground. 7
Reborn. 10
The Serpents Sting. 12
Give It Back, Devil!. 14
Tomorrow, About This Time 16
He Broke The Curse. 18
Oil Of The Lord. 20
Power Over The Enemy. 22
The Juniper Tree 24
Chain Of Bondage 26
The Rushing Wind. 28
When God Says No 30
Be Better, Not Bitter 32
A Penny For Your Soul. .34
Servants Of The Lord. 36
The Day Of The Cross 38
The Risen Lord 40
A Kind Word To Say 42
Gift Of Healing 44
A Prayer For You 46
The Gift Of Christmas 48
The Words We Speak 50
River Of Cream 52
Man-O-War 54
The Day Beckons 57

Jubilee In The Sky	58
To Reach The Throne Room	60
The Little Things	62
Everything You Do	64
The Morning Star Rises	66
Timeline	68
The Day And Hour Unknown	71
The Barren Wilderness	72
The Finish Line	74
Don't Envy The Sinners	76
Footsies With The Devil	78
Masterpiece	81
Get Back Up Again	82
Jealousy	84
Be A Blessing	86
You Ain't Lived Until You Give	89
Battlefield Of The Mind	90
Don't Laugh At The Leper	92
Don't Live On Tomorrow's Sunshine	94
Face The Wind	96
Towers To Self	98
Bind You Satan	101
Parable Of The Seed	102
When Morning Dawns	104

Stand Your Ground

Don't Run!
Stand your ground!
Don't let this world
kick you around.

In the eye of a storm
be still.
Let nothing push
you at will.

You're a son
of the most high.
Jesus is your
battle cry.

You have the
armor to defend.
Daring determination
to win.

Once the battle
has begun,
Evil forces
will turn and run.

Be bold determined
to get respect
and place your foot
on the devil's neck.

Don't Run!
Stand your ground!
Don't let this world
kick you around.

You're a son
of the most high.
Jesus is your
battle cry.
NO MATTER THE ODDS

Stand strong in the Lord
and never be afraid,
as a child of His
you will be saved.

You'll be victorious
no matter the odds,
stand on the Word
with trust in God.

Called into action
you'll have the resource,
coming against

any opposing force.

For the Lord's Promise
you can proclaim,
wait on Him
you'll not be ashamed.

When He speaks
the heavens will roar;
when He sends lightening
you'll begin to soar.

From the end of the earth,
smoke begins to rise,
overcoming the obstacles
no matter the size.

Call on His name
He will deliver,
as you walk waters
of the mightiest rivers.

For the Lord's Promise
you can proclaim,
wait on Him
you'll not be ashamed.

Reborn

There are times we're
trashed with life's litter
and love's defection
can make us bitter.

When our hopes
and dreams become extinct,
each step we take
we begin to sink.

When our goals
nurtured, reach rejection
we then must stop
for thorough introspection.

With renewed vigor
and the Lord's strength,
we'll rise again
without giving an inch.

We'll dry our tears
where there was defeat
reclaim the ground
we lost in retreat.

We're stronger and wiser
from this tribulation
replaced disappointment
with a new determination.

Battered but not beaten
tattered but didn't tear,
we didn't give up
because Jesus was there.

There's now a rose
where there had been thorns
instead of despair
we have been reborn.

The Serpents Sting

Standing in the
center of the ring.
Fighting the fire
of the serpent's sting.

The Lord knows
what you can take.
He always allows
a way of escape.

When things close in
don't get concerned.
Heroes don't quit
in danger stand firm.

Then with God
you can be reconciled.
To grow in faith
takes effort and trial.

Come to the Lord
in true supplication.
In His time
He'll grant vindication.

Standing in the center of the ring.
Fighting the fire
of the serpent's sting.

The Lord knows
what you can take.
He always allows
a way of escape.

Give It Back, Devil!

It's time for us
to make a decree.

Give it back, Devil
it belongs to me!
Give it back, Devil
it belongs to me!
For God has given us the victory!

Give it back, give it back
it belongs to me!
Because God doesn't
want us in misery!

Give it back, give it back
it belongs to me!
Because God doesn't
want us in poverty!

Give it back, Devil
you've now been told.
For Jesus has broken
your demonic strongholds.

Give it back, give it back
Immediately!
For God will bring us
prosperity!

Give it back, give it back
Expediently!
For God will restore
our families!

Give it back, Devil
you've now been told.
For Jesus has broken
your demonic strongholds.

Tomorrow, About This Time

Tomorrow about this time
God's got something for you.
Tomorrow about this time
He'll make your dreams come true.

Raise your hands and praise Him
dance and sing about.
'Cause tomorrow about this time
you'll have reason to shout!

Tomorrow about this time
God has something to say.
Tomorrow about this time
He will make a way.

Revelation for your situation
so stay in the race.
Tomorrow about this time
you will see God's grace.

Tomorrow about this time
the work is already done.
Tomorrow about this time
the battle has been won.

Plead the blood of Jesus
the Devil is under your feet.
Tomorrow about this time
you'll have the victory!

He Broke The Curse

When things aren't right,
it could be worse.
Glory to God,
He broke the curse.

If there's confusion,
and I don't understand,
Praise Jesus! I still
have my hands.

If I feel let down
and want to cry,
I thank God
for giving me eyes.

If this wicked world
tries to bring defeat,
I still have a house
and something to eat.

If dreams I have
don't come true,
thank You, Jesus,
I still have You.

When things go wrong,
it could be worse.
Glory to God,
He broke the curse.

Oil Of The Lord

Idle words, foolish chatter.
The words we say really do matter.

Victory against Satan
are in words we choose.
Speak words of faith
you will never lose.

The Word of God cuts
like crackling thunder.
A piercing sword
splitting the soul asunder.

The Word of God
is your burning oil.
Food for your body
that will never spoil.
Words of the Lord
bring eternal life.
Power to overcome
what the world may entice.

It is Written, it is Written
words from Jesus' mouth
It is Written, it is Written
left the Devil in doubt.

It is Written, it is Written
will seal Hades' tomb
Oil of the Lord
will bring the Devil's doom.

Power Over The Enemy

Behold, we are given
power over the enemy,
for Jesus has set
the captive free.

As children of God
in one accord,
we call on the might
of our precious Lord.

We have been granted
this royal petition
to release my brothers
of demonic affliction.

You have now trespassed
on Holy Ground.
In the name of the Lord,
I cast you down.

To quench the fire
of burning coals
in the deepest
caverns of Sheol.

This Prince of Peace
is whom I trust.
Under His feet,
you've now been crushed.

The world of God
in strength and will,
and in His holiness,
I've now been sealed.

The Father commands
the legions to leave
by the blood of Jesus
of Calvary.

The Juniper Tree

Sitting by the Juniper tree,
praying to Jesus
to bring relief.

Satan in full
force is back
and has you under
an all-out attack.

There's no doubt
he wants control,
waging a war to
control your soul.

You pray to God
to get refreshed,
hurry up and get
me out of this mess.

But God was
never out of reach.
He had something
He wanted to teach.

Sitting by the
Juniper tree,
the Lord will make
a delivery.

Soon thereof
the anointing will flow,
saith the Lord:
Rise up and go!

Chain Of Bondage

You feel in control
when pleasure reigns
each passing day
tightens the chain.

When you lift that
bottle to take a drink
the hammer clamors
to add another link.

A perverse work uttered
cannot return
matches to the fire
your soul to burn.

Light a cigarette
puff on a smoke
a life of bondage
until you choke.

A corrosive heart
becomes a hardened callous,
contaminated from years
of envy and malice.

Years of bitterness
have become entrenched.
Foul odor of hatred
leaves a sickening stench.

Blinders of the world
control how you think
each sinful pleasure
adds another link.

There's no freedom
when carnal living reigns.
As time goes on,
it tightens the chain.

The Prince of the Earth
is whom you pay homage
blinded by the world
to the chain of bondage.

The Rushing Wind

Step over the line
leave it all behind
the adventure will begin.
Here comes the rushing Wind.

My mission is now clear
because His coming is near.
I've given up material living.
I'm prepared for spiritual giving.

My friends are now few.
I won't quit until it's through.
I don't hunger for acclaim;
my desire is not fortune or fame.

It's God in Whom I abide.
I don't lean to the other side.
There's no time to hesitate
or room to negotiate.

I have made the sacrifice
to serve my Lord, Jesus Christ.

Step over the line
leave it all behind
the adventure will begin.
Here comes the Rushing Wind.

When God Says No

When God says no,
don't get upset.
You're not meant
to have it yet.

When God says no,
there's something in mind.
Anger is only
a waste of time.

Be patient, let His
plan unfold
time to detour
down another road.

Turning you away
from getting burned,
bringing new knowledge
for you to learn.

Working on a design
you do not see,
arranging better things
for you to be.

When God says no,
you feel let down.
Keep the faith,
you'll receive the crown.

Be Better, Not Bitter

Let me describe
how it can affect
you and I.

Being bitter is
bad judgement.
Do not hold on
to this torment.

It is poison,
it is not Christ,
will turn a loving soul into ice.

It never accomplished
any desire,
except to consume
a person like fire.

If it comes, perchance
here's how to change
the circumstance.

Being bitter is your enemy
after the B, change
the I to E to have
victory.

The Lord will
then be pleased
and will rain
upon your blessings.

Never give in
to bitterness,
it is better
to have contentment.

For being bitter
is the enemy
after the B change the I to E
to have victory.

A Penny For Your Soul

Can the Devil pay
a penny for your soul?
Or are your treasures
in the City of Gold?

Would a large ruby
make a good sale,
make him close
his bid from hell?

Or could the price
of a sapphire
put your soul in
the lake of fire?

All it would take
to raise the price
is for you to
serve Jesus Christ.

Then the Devil
would close the lid
on his efforts
to make a bid.

Otherwise, there's one
guarantee:
your soul can be
bought for a penny.

Can the devil pay
a penny for your soul?
Or are your treasures
in the City of Gold?

All it would take
to raise the price
is for you to
serve Jesus Christ.

Servants Of The Lord

Hear me, America!
All you distant nations.
The Lord called me
long before creation.

When there was darkness
I hid in His loins.
I cried, "Abba, Father,"
when the universe was formed.

I was with Him
long before my birth
I saw Him set the heavens,
the foundation of the Earth.

He made the clouds,
the depths of the deep.
I praise Him for the
horizons on the sea.

I stood on the mountains
when He put them in place,
looked in awe as He
smoothed out their base.

I stepped back and
watched the hills and springs,
cried tears of joy
when He made living things.

The blast of His nostrils
made day and night,
then He rested to make
sure things were right.

Bless the Lord,
Who made heaven and Earth,
called us His servants
years before our birth.

We were chosen
long before creation,
the Lord called
and granted our salvation.

The Day Of The Cross

Though many loved Him,
He was widely despised.
It led to the cross
to be crucified.

With a crown of thorns
upon His head,
the ground beneath Him
was crimson red.

They mocked Him
spit on Him as He walked by
the cross of the world,
tears of blood in His eyes.

No beauty or majesty
to be esteemed,
but because He died,
we have been redeemed.

By oppression and judgment,
He was taken away,
crushed for our iniquities
with nothing to say.

For our transgressions,
He died for our sins.
He endured humiliation,
He would rise again.
He would rise again.

The Risen Lord

They all came
to look and see
our risen Lord,
the Prince of Peace.

The huge stone
was rolled aside.
His body was gone
because He's alive.

Through all the torture,
agony, and pain,
degradation, death,
nakedness, and shame.

He chose to
die by the cross
to bring atonement
for all the lost.

Blood of the lamb,
as it slowly dripped,
brought words of
forgiveness from His lips.

He did these things
for you and me,
so we may live
eternally.

Our risen Lord,
the Prince of Peace,
He has risen, come and see.
He is alive for you and me.

A Kind Word To Say

It begins each morning
of every day.
The people we meet
have a kind word to say.

That person you met
life might be hard,
it could be through you
she hears of the Lord.

The little ole lady
you met on the street,
turned her life to
victory from defeat.

Every time you offered
a listening ear,
gave them hope
where there had been fear.

The young boy
you told, "do your best,
one day you'll
be a great success."

He needed that
to finish his goal.
He'll help someone
'cause what he was told.

It begins each morning
of every day.
The people we meet
have a kind word to say.

The man you meet
life might be hard,
could be through you
he hears from the Lord.

Gift Of Healing

In the name of Jesus,
as I pray now
healing will come
where I have been bound.

Spirit of infirmity,
you must go.
I rebuke all illness,
for the Word says so.

Because my request
is before the throne,
in His tender mercy,
all sickness is gone.

I come against the Devil,
the diabolical ploy,
his deadly mission
of kill, steal, destroy.

Our God is great,
I call on His name,
forever protect us
from all kinds of pain.

Our glorious Jesus,
who has given
His truth, grace,
and eternal provision.

The Holy Spirit
dwelling in me
has removed the world's
impurities.

By His stripes,
I've now been healed
because His presence
has been revealed.

Thank you, Jesus,
for cleansing my soul,
bringing me healing,
and making me whole.

A Prayer For You

I know life has
been unkind
and what you need
you simply can't find.

But I've prayed
a prayer for you.
God's wisdom and
grace will see you through.

I prayed for Jesus
to be so near,
so when He speaks,
His voice you'll hear.

I pray you'll feel
His gentle touch,
so the fires of life
won't burn as much.

I prayed to Jesus
to be at your side,
whatever you need
grace will provide.

I prayed this trial
will make you strong,
and through it all,
you're not alone.

The Gift Of Christmas

The holidays have come.
Hear the Christmas bells
singing praises to the King,
the child Emanuel.

The star's shining brilliance
almost seems alive
brings light to the world.
His birthday has arrived.

See the people caroling
early in the night
as the children lay sleeping,
what a beautiful sight.

Coming of the Kingdom
brings hope it seems,
and peace on Earth
is no longer a dream.

All God's creations
stand upon the Earth
sing unto the heavens
to celebrate His birth.

The holidays have come.
Hear the Christmas bells
singing praises to the King,
the child Emanuel.

The Words We Speak

Without much thought
or conscious attempt,
we can show strong
feelings of contempt.

Not caring enough
to fully realize
someone's feelings
have been pulverized.

Like broken glass
never fully restored,
the person will never
be the same as before.

If wisdom and goodness
our conversation lacks,
we're not sure how
a person will react.

Fruit of the Spirit
should be on display
godly behavior and the
words we say.

A broken life
in the garbage heap.
Jesus can save
by the words we speak.

River Of Cream

He takes foolish things
to confound the wise.
He chooses those
the world despised.

Jesus befriends
the social outcast,
comforts the many
the world has passed.

He'll change your life
if things seem bleak,
humble the proud
while raising the meek.

Those in anguish
lonely and dejected
used, abuse, cursed,
disrespected.

Fatherless, homeless,
and dispossessed,
the faint of heart
whose soul is oppressed.

He'll bring you
to a peaceful stream,
a river flowing with
honey and cream.

He takes foolish things
to confound the wise,
He chooses those
the world despised.

Jesus befriends
the social outcast,
comforts the many
the world has passed.

Man-O-War

With sword in hand
carrying His shield
in battle against evil,
I'll never yield.

I'll fight always
wherever I'm deployed,
battling against Satan
until he's destroyed.

The armor of God
from head to feet
attacking always
to bring his defeat.

We'll conquer his
forces with authority.
The captains of host,
we claim victory.

As Man-O-War
carrying God's shield
against the evil one
I'll never yield.

God's mighty army
will always prevail
we'll drive the demon hoards
into the pits of hell.

The Day Beckons

I open my arms to the day,
waiting, silently, patiently
in expectancy for a gift from God.
His gift to me,
my gift to Him, can hardly restrain itself.

Running mildly, then wildly
like a child running
rampant in a candy store.

Where grace, faith, and hope
bounce upon me bountifully,
and in their reflective wisdom,
I will get a glimpse of
eternal mysteries
and eternal purpose.

While gazing into the mind
of the universe
and touching
the hand of God.

Jubilee In The Sky

Prepare yourselves
the day is drawing nigh
when we all meet God
at the Jubilee in the sky.

There will be singing, shouting
the dead will also rise
sing Glory Hallelujah
sing it by and by.

On that blessed day,
we'll see Jesus eye to eye,
King of Kings
at the Jubilee in the sky.

Families are together
in this jubilation.
Children are enjoying
the heavenly sensation.

The Lord's banquet
by the crystal sea.
All those present
sing glory, glory, glory.

Prepare yourselves,
the day is drawing nigh
when we all meet God
at the Jubilee in the sky.

There will be singing, shouting
the dead will also rise
sing Glory Hallelujah
sing it by and by.

The Book of Praise

To Reach The Throne Room

Come into the
Throne of Grace
bring your prayers
to this holy place.

The alter of your heart
petition your views
your silent dreams
will reach the throne room.

He'll split your burdens
like He parted the sea
you'll rise above
all your enemies.

He'll seal your
wounds with healing balm
if life is a tempest
the Lord brings a calm.

When hearing your request
by this you'll know
the nod of His head
the winds will blow.

Like a hurricane
coming through the clouds
when He appears
the mountains must bow.

He'll crush the enemy
and break their strength
who can wage war
when the Lord's your defense.

Come unto the
Throne of Grace
bring your prayers
to this holy place.

The alter of your heart
petition your views
your silent dreams
will reach the Throne Room.

The Little Things

There is a wilderness
you must go through
for God to work His
destiny in you.

Don't neglect the small
seemingly insignificant things
the drudgery of everyday
or life's routine.

What's before you
may not look too grand
but you're still in the palm
of God's mighty hand.

Don't take for granted
any mundane thing,
it's from this well
that greatness will spring.

To be part of
God's great commission
you must go through
a period of prolonged submission.

In a bad situation
that you may despise
your future could be working
right before your eyes.

Everything You Do

Everything you do
affects someone else
no man lives
among himself.

You need to watch
what you say
your words could
lead others astray.

Participate only
in edifying discussions,
so there won't be
unexpected repercussions.

Remember others look
up to you
are watching/imitating
everything you do.

Whatever is done
could affect a kid,
he'll soon do it
because you did.

Everything you do
affects someone else
no man lives
among himself.

Watch what you do
and what you say
immoral behavior
leads others astray.

The Morning Star Rises

Changes in our lives
can quite suddenly
bring upon us
great catastrophe.

When there's no income
children to be fed
a normal family life
is looking pretty dead.

All these dilemmas
have you feeling drained,
weighing you down
with an earthly chain.

Answers are hard
in our human limitations,
finding ways to overcome
this tremendous decimation.

Through your wounded heart,
keep the Spirit's flow
the answers will come
His greatness you'll know.

Come to quiet waters
pastures of tender herbs
it will renew your hopes
your spirit will be served.

Your help is at hand
bringing needed adoration
to lift your broken spirit
with faith's affirmation.

The morning star rises
bringing help to His own
the everlasting Christ,
who reigns on the throne.

Timeline

The Lord will
always let you know
in what direction
you need to go.

As you live,
then you'll find
the world moves
on a timeline.

If your choices
lead into a wall
and every step
you trip and fall.

Like a train
you're now off track
time for Jesus
to put you back.

Then when you
follow His direction,
you're within the Lord's
protection.

Because you are
now in God's will
His plan for you
is being fulfilled.

Stay on course
and you will find
the seasons and reasons
for the timeline.

The Day And Hour Unknown

The day and the
hour is unknown
in the twinkling of an eye
He'll be gone.

The Lord will
come without a sign
will you be taken
or left behind?

Be faithful Christian
servant, be wise
listen always,
watch the skies.

Pray fervently
to hear His voice
then you can be
His prize choice.

The Lord will come
without a sign.
Will you be taken
or left behind?

The Barren Wilderness

As God's People
there's too much bigotry,
back-biting, judgmental,
out-of-control hypocrisy.

Some leaders in jail
others on trial,
Christians continue
self-serving lifestyles.

The world views religion
as a bygone fable,
the media has branded
us with unsavory labels.

We're called into question
whom we serve
unfortunately, a perception
Christians deserve.

It's time to stop
this moral pollution,
we as the church
are the solution.

We won't accept
moral compromise
distortions, half-truths,
myths, and lies.

The world needs to see
we're leaders of light
the Holy Spirit guiding
we'll do what's right.

Living by the Word,
we will be blessed
rescue will come
in the barren wilderness.

The Finish Line

Many people wish
they could change their life
do things different
to make it right.

If only you could
start all over again
you wouldn't have lived
this life of sin.

You would listen
to others' advice
since you didn't,
you're paying the price.

Jesus will take you
at this place
and give you strength
to finish the race.

He'll pull you up
from being last
like a champion
you'll then run fast.

You can't turn back
the hands of time
but you can sprint
to the finish line.

Don't Envy The Sinners

Don't envy the sinner
or covet his ways,
calamity will come
and end his days.

Do not accept
his way of life,
or do what's wrong
when you know what's right.

Don't judge others
by what they possess
or kill yourself striving
for worldly success.

Like a castle
built on the sand
all come to ruin
that's made by man.

Living your life
to gain respect
a path seems right
whose end is death.

Don't envy the sinner
or desire his taste
his ambitions
will come to waste.

Footsies With The Devil

Footsies with the Devil
it's not for fun
if he appears
it's time to run.

He will come
with a malicious grin
whatever it takes
he wants to be friends.

He'll really try
to make you believe
you're missing the twin:
malice and greed.

You'll be convinced
things aren't just,
so coming along
are envy and lust.

You'll become his
own personal toy
his ultimate aim:
Kill/Destroy.

Satan's goals
are stumbling blocks
he will build them
until you drop.

He'll offer you
dinner of stinking meat
and deceitful dessert
of bittersweet.

He's holding behind
his back a knife
waiting for the moment
to take your life.

Masterpiece

The sun rays reflecting
for all to see
a kaleidoscope
that created a masterpiece.

Replaying the day
like a movie screen
mountains in the clouds
whose appearance is serene.

A stairway to the clouds
which defies time
red and orange colors
I wish I could climb.

Absorbing the splendor
for all to see
the Lord of hosts
displays His masterpiece.

Get Back Up Again

When running the race,
and you really want to win,
if you fall to your knees,
Get Back Up Again.

When at the starting line
place your feet in the blocks
rise up, run the race,
and don't you ever stop.

Though they jeer you, hit you,
and knock you to the ground,
raise your head up
when you hear that trumpet sound.

Let nothing stop your dream
or get in your way,
push mountains aside,
turn night into day.

Scale heights if you must,
cross canyons if you can,
reach beyond the clouds,
grab stars with your hands.

Some days, it's an inch
other days, it's a mile
but always moving forward
and progressing all the while.

Though they fear you, hit you,
and knock you to the ground,
raise your head up
when you hear that trumpet sound.

When the race gets started,
and you're determined to win,
if you fall to your knees,
"Just Get Back Up Again."

Jealousy

Jealousy is
the hidden sin,
if it appears
can bring your end.

Of all feelings
this is the worst,
the end result
is an evil curse.

Your inner soul
will become oppressed,
fill your days with
the demon of distress.

Evil abominations
will fill your heart,
vice grips of malice
will rip you apart.

Death and destruction
are in your eyes,
the torch of hate
burns inside.

Jealousy is cold
as the grave,
within these walls
none are saved.

When it comes
to dominate,
pray to Jesus
before it's too late.

The power of jealousy
is strong and real,
call on the Lord
because it can kill.

Be A Blessing

Be a blessing to people
who come your way,
in the things you do
and the words you say.

Helping a fellow brother
by planting a seed,
help the hurting
by fulfilling his need.

When helping someone,
it comes back to you.
You become like Christ
helping dreams come true.

When seeing your face,
their soul's at rest.
You've become their own
answered prayer request.

Derwin Boyd

Be a blessing to people
who come your way,
in the things you do
and the words you say.

You become like Christ,
helping dreams come true,
when blessing others,
it comes back to you.

You Ain't Lived Until You Give

When helping someone,
you've begun to live.
Real joy in life
comes when you give.

The Lord says give,
and give unto me.
What you do in secret
is rewarded openly.

When you give unto others,
God's promise unfolds.
You'll reap Heaven's treasures
to be rewarded sevenfold.

When giving to the least
you give unto me.
By helping needy people
obtain the victory.

When you give unto others,
God's promise unfolds.
You'll reap heaven's treasures
to be rewarded sevenfold.

Battlefield Of The Mind

The mind is
a major battlefield
where the flesh and the world
attack at will.

In the Spirit
the battle is unceasing
Hound of Hell
never releasing.

To seek control
of your imagination
with the fiery darts
of tormenting temptations.

This tug of war
of to and fro
the Spirit, the flesh
wanting a foothold.

Every thought then
must be scrutinized
it is God
or Satan disguised.

Wage war in the Lord
with the Belt of Truth
victory is certain
with mind renewed.

You will withstand
what the world can impose
be able to destroy
ungodly strongholds.

Wage war in the Lord,
you won't be blind
victory is certain
in your soul and mind.

Don't Laugh At The Leper

Don't laugh at the Leper
because he's deformed
as a son of God
for a purpose, he was born.

Don't shun your neighbor
if he has AIDS
in the Father's image,
he was also made.

Don't pass the crippled
or overlook the insane
have compassion, my brother
pray for their pain.

Don't treat the old
with benighted neglect,
let them see mercy
with love and respect.

When showing kindness
to the least of these,
we're in Christ's service
recognizing their needs.

When you called Jesus,
He didn't laugh
but came to you
because you asked.

Don't be indifferent
if people are deranged,
or turn the other way
if they seem a little strange.

Don't laugh at the Leper
before your life is through
as the world keeps turning
one day that could be you.

Don't Live On Tomorrow's Sunshine

I don't live on
borrowed time,
don't live today
on tomorrow's sunshine.

Even though the sky
may be clear,
in just a moment
a storm could appear.

I'm not a prisoner
to past dreams,
my hold of the present
is not extreme.

I don't get depressed
or in a rut,
what could have happened
with a little luck?

What has happened
don't make me sad,
I don't daydream on
what I could have had.

There's only one thing
I do understand,
my future is held
by the Son of Man.

So I turn my head
and train my eyes
to keep going forward
until I reach the prize.

I don't live on
borrowed time,
don't live today
on tomorrow's sunshine.

So turn your head
and train your eyes
to keep going forward
until you reach the prize.

Face The Wind

Never abandon
the ship too soon
in stormy waters
of a typhoon.

Take a sounding
face the wind
closely examine
the situation you're in.

The waters are deep
and you're off course
with the anchor of faith
make the Lord your source.

Lighten the ship
discard the load
worldly burdens
will take their toll.

Survive these waters
priorities are straight
you're now becoming
what God wants to make.

Into the horizon
the sky is clear
you'll reach the goal
the shore is near.

Towers To Self

Building monuments
you want others to see,
showing the world
your new identity.

Glittering glamour,
a new house and clothes,
rings on each finger,
diamonds on your nose.

You must own the best,
drive a new sports car,
so the world will think
you're some superstar.

You strive and strive
for that all-important job,
those you call friends
are nothing more than snobs.

A monument to self
to show all things achieved,
you don't want Jesus
it's more things you need.

Objects and things
become gods in our lives,
we build these idols
to show others we've arrived.

This Tower of Babel
will stretch to the sky,
it's all left behind
on the day you die.

Bind You Satan

I bind you SATAN by the Son of Light,
I cast you back into eternal night.

I shackle your demons in His Holy Name,
I relieve those who are in spiritual pain.

In the name of Jesus, go back to the pit.
By the power of His spirit, return to the abyss.

I call on the Father in this desperate hour,
to destroy your stronghold, principalities, and powers.

To those in bondage, you are now free.
By the power of the cross, the demons must flee.

May the suffering you caused come to an end,
and a heavenly breeze cool the scorching wind.

Parable Of The Seed

There are many times
when the seed is sown,
it will remain for a moment,
then it is gone.

If the seed is sown
in a rocky place,
you'll lose the blessing
of our Lord's good grace.

If trouble comes and
you fall away or
the things of this world
become a tidal wave.

These things happen
to make you choke,
and the word disappears
like a puff of smoke.

But if the word
then falls upon a rock,
Satan will destroy you
with stumbling blocks.

Find good ground
for your seed to grow
like a tree by a stream
in strength it will grow.

When Morning Dawns

When morning dawns,
we'll bless You.
Before the day begins,
we offer up our prayers
with the rising sun.

The hope for our world
is in Your awesome deeds.
You quiet the warring nations
and still the mighty seas.

There's strength and glory
when morning and evening fade,
we hear thundering power
in the roaring waves.

All fear Your wonders
the things You've ordained,
the meadows clothed in splendor
the valley's flowing with grain.

All the earth bows
singing praises to Your name,
how awesome Your creation
how refreshing is Your rain.

When morning dawns,
we'll bless You
with abundant praise,
bringing songs of joy
when morning and evening fade.

When morning dawns,
we'll sing
about all Your awesome deeds,
Your powers formed the mountains
and stilled the mighty seas.

CPSIA information can be obtained
at www.ICGtesting.com
Printed in the USA
BVHW072116151222
654331BV00023B/1546